MINEHEAD – PORT OF CALL

The History of Minehead Pier

and

Paddle Steamers

Charles Atkins

Motley Geekery

MINEHEAD – PORT OF CALL

ISBN: 978-0-9929197-0-2

Published by: Motley Geekery

43 Emmetts Park, Ashburton, Devon TQ13 7DB

www.motleygeekery.co.uk

For Stanley and Elizabeth
Jack, Marjorie, Rosie, Alice and Minnie
All pier and steamer enthusiasts – past and present

And finally to Sean without whose help and encouragement
this book would not have seen the light of day.

'Where Tall ships and seafarers plied trade across the sea,
And weatherbeaten fishermen spread nets out on the quay.
Those times are past, now pleasure cruisers ride the ocean waves,
To serve the trippers longing for adventure that he craves.
The romance of those far off days is easy brought to bear.
By quayside rails, in quiet mood, salt breezes, shingled shore.'

In Exmoor Countrie
by
Penny Housden

1 - Minehead Pier and Paddle Steamer

One of the murals at Townsend House, Minehead by the artist Ted Borrett

CONTENTS

CONTENTS

INTRODUCTION

For over 500 years men have sailed into the harbour guided by the light at the rood loft window in St. Michael's Church tower. Carved above the East window on the outside wall c1529 is a prayer for Minehead's fishermen of long ago *"We pray to Jesu and Mary – send our neighbours safety."*

The earliest mention of a harbour dates from 1380 when weirage dues were collected for its maintenance. Forty years later a 'juttie' was built by the Luttrell family – referred to as 'le weir' – at the mouth of the Bratton stream joining the sea at the end of Blenheim Road. Trade grew fast and Sir Hugh Luttrell had a new harbour built which increased the capacity which in turn attracted more vessels. By 1543, Minehead came second only to Bristol among the Channel ports.

In 1558 Queen Elizabeth I granted a Charter raising Minehead to Borough status with a Port Reeve and Council. Unfortunately numerous gales damaged the harbour and it was breached making it useable only by local fishermen. In 1604 King James withdrew the Charter and returned the 'overlordship' to the Luttrells.

In 1616 a new harbour was built along the shore to the West which is the structure we see today. In 1682 it was strengthened by bringing in a number of large rocks from Greenaleigh Point, some weighing more than a ton were floated by means of casks then piled on the beach behind the harbour to break the force of the waves, where they can still be seen.

By 1712 the harbour was twice the size with repairs to it in 1846 and 1870. Earlier in 1862, because of navigational problems of the Bristol Channel and criticisms of both Minehead and Watchet harbours, it was suggested a new harbour be constructed at Greenaleigh using Gypsum from Blue Anchor to make concrete for the underwater work. The idea was never taken up.

By the end of the century Mineheads reputation as a health spa and holiday resort was rapidly growing. A pier was built in 1900 to allow pleasure steamers to call independent of the tides. Paddle steamers of the Red, White and Yellow funnel fleets called regularly at the new Victorian pier. Sometimes as many as five steamers came to the landing stage on any one tide and bringing thousands of visitors to Minehead during the summer season.

In 1939 the pier was removed on instructions from the War Office.

CHAPTER ONE

The Case For Building A Pier

Steamers had been calling regularly at Minehead since the 1830s when the P.S. (Paddle Steamer) *Lady Rodney* of the Bristol General Steam Navigation Company made the first recorded landing. In 1834 a meeting took place at the Wellington Hotel, chaired by Mr W C Trevelyn, to raise capital of £4,000 in £25 shares, to float a company to run a Steam Packet service between Minehead and Watchet to Cardiff and Bristol. As only half the money was raised the project was shelved. From about 1850, a local visionary, Richard Date of Watchet had the idea of hiring steam tugs from Cardiff and Bristol for regular summer trips in the Bristol Channel. These trips were advertised in the *West Somerset Free Press* and by hand-bills and attracted large crowds to sample a day at sea.

During the 1860s and 1870s, Date advertised trips on such vessels as the *Earl of Dunraven, Earl of Jersey, Neath Abbey, Stevenson* and *Defiance.* Crossing to Wales for the day was common as was collecting passengers from Wales and bringing them to Minehead and Watchet. The descriptions of these tugs were set out in the most flowery terms making these little working vessels sound like luxury cruisers.

2 - P.S. Bonnie Doon

A group of speculative Bristol businessmen, chartered the P.S. *Bonnie Doon* to run excursions in the Bristol Channel for the 1886 season. Their actions sowed the seed which eventually resulted in the birth of P & A Campbell's White Funnel fleet of pleasure steamers that served the area for close on a century. In 1887 and 1888 the first paddle steamer *Waverley* was chartered by the same Bristol syndicate for similar reasons.

3 - P.S. *Waverley*

By the early 1890s the White Funnel fleet was providing regular steamer services between other Bristol Channel ports and Minehead. In September 1893 the P.S. *Scotia* entered Minehead harbour for the first time carrying almost 400 passengers from Cardiff and was the subject of great local interest. On Whit Monday 1894, the *West Somerset Free Press* reported that between 1,000 and 1,500 trippers had disembarked from South Wales. In order to extend the times when passengers could embark and disembark at Minehead, the local Squire, Mr Geoffrey Fownes Luttrell, initiated a scheme to build a pier. In July 1894, surveys were made and soundings taken at a spot to the west of the old harbour. At a special meeting called by Minehead residents in August it was agreed to support Mr Luttrell in forming a company to build a pier.

An application for a Provisional Order (outline planning permission) was deposited on 28 November 1894, in accordance with the Grand Pier & Harbour Act 1861, for consideration by the Board of Trade. By April 1895 Mr Luttrell, of Dunster Castle, had obtained permission from the Board of Trade to build a promenade pier at Minehead, with pavilion, saloon, baths and reading room. Parliamentary orders made by the Board of Trade over plans for a new pier and harbour at Minehead were given a Second Reading in the House of Lords in June 1895. Good news travelled fast. TUC delegates at Cardiff in September visited Minehead on a cruise in the Bristol Channel. The party included John Burns MP and the Mayor of Cardiff, Mr Carey.

BOARD OF TRADE

➤ Session, 1895. ◄

MINEHEAD NEW PIER AND HARBOUR.

APPLICATION FOR PROVISIONAL ORDER.

4- Planning Application 1895

August Bank Holiday 1897 brought vast numbers of visitors to Minehead. The morning steamer alone brought between 300 and 400 passengers. The Minehead & West Somerset races on the sands attracted a huge number from Cardiff who came over on the P.S. *Lady Margaret.* The first excursion of the season was organised by none other than Mr R S Date. The P.S. *Waverley* arrived at Minehead harbour from Cardiff with 100 passengers who landed for the day and the boat took about the same number over to Cardiff. 'The day being beautifully fine, it was a very pleasant excursion'.

Design and Planning

John James Webster, an eminent engineer who specialised in bridge construction and who had earlier designed Dover and Bangor (Garth) piers, was approached to design a new pier and harbour for Minehead. As expected, he was very precise in his specifications. The pier was to be built 21 yards northeast of the lifeboat house and 11 yards northwest from the corner of Thomas Kent Riddler's storehouse. It should extend seaward in a northeast direction for a distance of 230 yards, be 24 feet wide expanding to 76 feet at its head and be 20 feet above high water at ordinary spring tides and to have four landing platforms. Later, in a letter dated 29 November 1900, he wrote expressing concerns about the siting of a new lifeboat house. He recommended it should not be less than 40 feet from the building to the edge of the sea bank (shingle ridge) so not to spoil the approach to the pier.

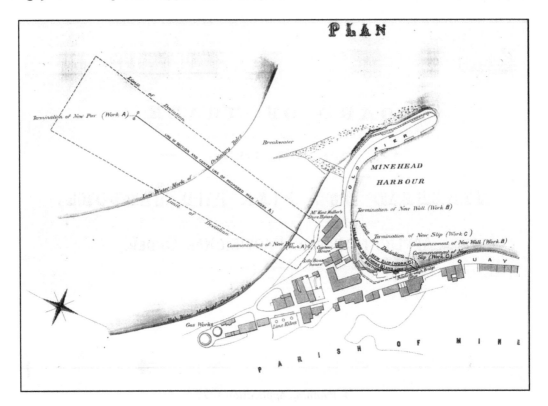

5 - Plan of the Pier

Meeting the Cost

As the structure of the pier was to be unostentatious and only serve a functional purpose, for example, to allow steamer passengers to embark and disembark conveniently rather than accommodate entertainment, the cost would be a modest £12,000.

In a letter to Mr Luttrell, Mr John Davis of Ponsford, Joyce and Davis, solicitors at Williton, gave details of how the capital would be raised for completion of the new pier and harbour wall.

		£
Mr R H Holman[1], Topsham	- land	3,000
Messrs Frowde	- shares	3,000
F Hancock, Wiveliscombe	- shares	2,000
Mr G F Luttrell	- shares	2,000
Messrs P & A Campbell	- shares	1,000
Local subscribers	- shares	1,000
		12,000

At a meeting of shareholders and other interested parties in the Esplanade Hotel on 3 March 1899, the Minehead Pier Company was formed, with Mr John Carey elected as Chairman of the directors.

6 - The Esplanade Private Hotel

[1] Mr Holman was an uncle of Vivien Leigh the actress who starred opposite Clarke Gable in the film *Gone with the wind.* His grandfather was a Master Mariner as well as a shipbuilder and owner. He Founded the West of England Marine Insurance Association in 1922.

Building the New Pier

Once the Pier Order had been granted by Parliament in 1895 and the Minehead Pier Company formed in 1899, pressure was on to get the project under way. Contracts were let and awarded to Messrs A Penny & Co., of London to build the pier and landing stages and to H W Pollard of Bridgwater to construct the approach road, harbour wall and slipway. The Resident Engineer was Mr L Savory.

7 -Workmen building the pier

This photograph shows the pier under construction from the drawings prepared by J J Webster in 1894. The original photograph used to hang in the back room of the Pier Hotel above the 'penny-in-the-slot' automatic piano that so many generations had poured beer into, that it sounded nothing like a piano.

CHAPTER TWO

Opening Day

Even before the official opening of the pier, Messrs Campbell announced they would begin their cross-channel service between Barry and Minehead on 20 May, in preparation for Whit week. They were soon running a daily service between Cardiff and Minehead and to Ilfracombe and other North Devon places several times a week.

8 – Minehead Pier staff. Harry Hole, proprietor of the Pier Hotel, 2nd Left, Mrs Fred Harrison and Capt. Smith, 2nd Right

The *West Somerset Free Press* described the formal opening of the pier, which took place on Saturday 25 May 1901 at 10.30 am with these words:

> *'Mr George Fownes Luttrell Esq., of Dunster Castle, and Lord of the Manor of Minehead, formally opened the New Promenade Pier at Minehead. The advisability of having a pier at Minehead is a subject that has been before the minds of the public of Minehead for years past, and opinion has been sharply divided on the subject...the pier is an accomplished fact and Minehead, for the summertime at least, is in daily contact with South Wales...'*

Mr Luttrell emphasised that Minehead welcomed its neighbours from across the Channel and offered the hand of friendship accordingly. Tribute was paid to the excellent White Funnel Fleet of paddle-steamers operated by P & A Campbell Ltd. that were to serve Minehead, and as the pier was formally declared open P.S. *Glen Rosa* came into view from across the Bristol Channel, and duly landed the first passengers at the pier.

Much celebrations and merry-making followed that day, and as well as hearing of 'friendly invasions from over the water', invited guests, including local dignitaries, enjoyed the 'recherché repast' provided for them at the nearby 'Hotel Metropole.

Other steamers called that day on various excursions including P.S. *Ravenswood, Westward Ho!* and *Waverley*. At one point three steamers lay alongside together at the new landing stage.

9 - Hotel Metropole – before the extension dome on the right

10 -P.S. Ravenswood with two funnels before her 1911 refit

11 - A photograph of the new pier taken by W G Hole shortly after the official opening by Mr G F Luttrell on 25 May 1901. The bunting flags can still be seen at the head of the pier where the opening ceremony took place. The P.S. Bonnie Doon is seen approaching the higher landing stage.

12 - *Another photograph by W G Hole showing the intricate pattern of the new pier's superstructure before the kiosk and shelter were added mid-way. The tide is calm with hardly a ripple. Washing can be seen drying on the shingle and two gasometers tucked in under the lee of the hill. Ketches can be seen at the old stone jetty, far right. A pleasure steamer has arrived to take on passengers.*

13 - *Launch of the new lifeboat George Leicester, c1902*

The following year, 1902 saw the launch of Minehead's first official lifeboat the *George Leicester* from the shingle ridge in front of the newly constructed lifeboat house. The boat was hauled off the ridge with the help of a line from the bow to the new pier. A large crowd came to witness the event from the beach and one can assume a similar number watched from the pier itself.

The *George Leicester* was a 35-foot Liverpool type Thames non-self-righting lifeboat, powered by sail and 12 oarsmen. It was built for £967 and paid for from a gift from Mrs Elizabeth Leicester of Bayswater, London. During its service period (December 1901 to August 1927) it saved 23 lives.

Daily Steamer Service

In March 1903, it was agreed that a daily steam boat service between Minehead and Barry would be discontinued in the summer in favour of a twice daily service between Minehead and Cardiff which it was felt would be much appreciated. Only exigencies of the tide stood in the way of the double service on every day.

Late Arrival

A storm of hurricane force tore through the entire district causing enormous damage everywhere. At Minehead there was no such serious damage as might have been expected. However, owing to broken wires messages could not be sent from vessels in the Bristol Channel, causing much anxiety when a Campbell's boat, with eight passengers on board, was late arriving at the pier.

In June 1903, possibly the largest monkfish ever seen on the Somerset coast was caught in Minehead harbour. The fish of a flat bodied kind, was five feet long and two feet eight inches broad.

Man Overboard

On 7 May 1904 the *West Somerset Free Press* reported a sad event occurring on the P.S. *Waverley* whilst on a cruise in the Channel. Some passengers sitting behind the saloon noticed a man stand on one of the seats at the rail of the vessel then suddenly disappear over the side into the water. A lifeboat was launched but after a half hour, the search was called off. Apparently, the man was travelling alone, no-one knew him or could remember how he was dressed.

Addition of Kiosk and Shelter

During 1907-8 a kiosk and shelter were added to the pier. Since opening day there had been many complaints from passengers arriving and departing during inclement weather, because there was no cover for those with luggage along the entire 230 yard length of the pier. Imagine what it must have been like in a brisk nor'westerly breeze!

14 - The Pier, Minehead

This picture by Hartmann c1907 shows the kiosk a third of the way along the pier, above the second stanchion. The luggage trolley rails can also be seen running up through the centre from the entrance to the pier head and the P.S. Bonnie Doon, lovingly known by the locals as Bonnie Break Doon, has just arrived.

15- The Pier, Minehead, from the Knight Collection c1908 is a view, taken from the front of the lifeboat house, of the pier entrance and the newly built kiosk. Passengers are disembarking from a steamer at the lower level and a horse-drawn carriage is waiting for hire – extreme right.

41410. Minehead. Pier & Red Funnel Steamer.

16 - The P.S. Devonia arriving and leaving Minehead pier. This photograph taken in 1910 shows 'her' in the Barry Railway Company colours with red funnels, she was later sold to P & A Campbell's in December 1911. The pier looking magnificent with the new shelter straddling the mid section and ready to receive passengers from across the channel.

17 - Photograph by local photographer Alfred Vowles shows the pier extending out into the bay beyond the harbour and the steamer in Campbell's colours (White funnels) just leaving.

Spiders Web

In a *Visitors List Publication* 1902 the pier is described as:

'a light, strong structure, resembling in the distance a spider's web spun in the shelter of the Quay, which effectually hides it from the sea front. It runs out into deep water, and emerges as it does from the shelter of the North Hill, it makes an excellent promenade, affording bracing breezes at its extremity. The view from the pier head with the magnificent mass of the North Hill looming overhead and the distant country to the eastward, is beautiful.'

18 - Photograph published by J Stevens of the Strand c1908 illustrates the completed pier with the addition of a shelter across the mid section.

19 - The Pier from Greenaleigh path. An early Francis Frith picture of 1908 shows the shelter and an excellent view of the four landing stages at the pier head. An Edwardian couple, on the right, are probably making their way to Greenaleigh for a cream tea.

Pier Tariff

In accordance with the Minehead Pier & Harbour Act 1895, the following charges were made:-

Passengers embarking	3d	A vessel landing	1d
Passengers landing	3d	Levies on luggage	
Walking for pleasure	2d	28 lbs	2d
Sedan chairs	4d	2 cwt	9d
Perambulators	3d	Bicycles and Tricycles	3d

Fresh water for the Pier 1s 6d per 100 gallons

Cream Teas and Junket

Day trippers (see definition) and holiday makers alike thought nothing of walking the mile and a half from the pier, through the woods, to quiet Greenaleigh Farm for a famous cream/junket tea. In 1900, Ada and Ted Rawle provided a 'very good' cream tea for one shilling and an early form of juke box provided a tune to listen to while you relaxed, for only one penny.

A peep of the sea from the tea gardens, Greenaleigh, Minehead.

20 - P.S. Lady Moyra passing Greenaleigh en-route to Ilfracombe after landing passengers from South Wales at the new pier.

Greenaleigh Farm lies one and a half miles northwest of Minehead harbour and is first mentioned in the 13th century. An old lease gave the owners sole rights to the fishing from Burgundy Chapel to the old stone jetty. Below the farm on the beach is a smugglers cave. In 1913, the French schooner *Moulette* ran aground in dense fog below, nearby West Myne farm.

Definition of a Day-Tripper c1909

A day tripper is 'a person who comes across the Bristol Channel from any of the South Wales ports, for half a day, and brings his nose-bag with him, or if it be a family party of trippers, a family hand-bag with provisions, including a bottle of beer for Mother and Father and milk for the children'. Thousands of these family parties came over by cheap steamboat excursions and may be observed on the sea-front at favoured resorts where they are apt to leave an offensive residium of their feasts behind them, in the shape of greasy paper and pieces of fat, as often as not upon the public seats. THOSE ARE DAY TRIPPERS. The unfortunate person, who clad in a light summer suit, has unwittingly sat upon a piece of ham fat left behind by one of these irresponsibles, hates the 'trippers' thereafter with a baleful intensity.

Charles G. Harper "The Somerset Coast"

Shared Ticket Office

21 - The Ticket Office

This street scene photographed in 1910 shows the ticket office, the notice by the wooden shed reads *'P & A CAMPBELL LTD. STEAMER OFFICE'*, just 4 years earlier in 1906 the same notice read *'BARRY, BRISTOL CHANNEL STEAMSHIP – RED FUNNEL'*. Opposite is the re-built Red Lion Hotel. The hill above the Red Lion is occupied by Henley Villa built for the Taunton builder A J Spiller. In 1920, the houses on the right-hand side of Quay Street, known as Lamb Cottages, were demolished and the road widened, with lawns sown and a pavement allowing pedestrians to stroll along the Promenade.

Choir Outing

In 1909, members of Rodhuish Church choir went on their annual outing, travelling by train to Minehead then by the P.S. Gwalia (Red Funnel) to Ilfracombe. Alex Gilberts company The Military Mummers played on the pier.

Votes for Women

The suffragette leader Mrs Emily Pankhurst held an election rally in the "Central Hall", Minehead on Saturday, 8th July 1911

CHAPTER THREE

Lull Before the Storm

22 - Pier and pleasure steamer c1914 C Kille

On the 15th February 1913 th AGM of the Minehead Pier Co, reported that that the extraordinarily wet summer of 1912 had caused a drop in pier tolls from £622 in 1911 to £437.

In April, Church collections were made for the Mansion House "Titanic Fund."

The 1914 season began normally with steamers calling regularly at the pier. The photograph above, taken by Mr Clement Kille, secretary of the Minehead Publicity Association, from the lifeboat house frontage shows the kiosk shelter and superstructure of the pier with the P.S. *Ravenswood* arriving fully laden with passengers.

On the 14th of February Mr G Brown, a Director of the Minehead Pier Co. and Mr C Kille, Honourable Secretary of the Minehead Improvements and Publicity Association, attended a Local Government Board enquiry at Burnham Sea into the application of Burnham UDC to borrow £10,000 to build a pier. There was strong opposition to the scheme from ratepayers. Mr Brown and Mr Kille gave evidence that there had been many fears over the scheme for building Minehead Pier, but that the development had meant a great deal to the town's improvement and attraction.

23 - M Salmet's aeroplane

In May, many watched an aeroplane, piloted by a Frenchman, M Salmet, land on the sands. This was an exhibition flight sponsored by the *Daily Mail*. M. Salmet was not the first airman to land at Minehead. This honour went to a Mr B C Hucks, who in 1910 touched down in a meadow near the sea front. He was flying a 50 h.p. monoplane (another demonstration machine provided by the *Daily Mail*) and had flown from Burnham on Sea in 22 minutes. In June, six Watchet boatmen put out to save the airman and a companion from drowning when the Daily Mail aeroplane came down in the sea off Watchet. They received a reward of £5 from the Daily Mail and a like sum from M Salmet and his companion, but only after Mr N.L. Hole had "taken up the cudgels" on their behalf. Of the £10, £1 was given for the use of the hobblers boat, so that the rescue men had 30s each.

On the 30th of May the P.S. *Glen Usk*, latest of P&A Campbell's pleasure steamers, arrived at Bristol from Troon where she was built. She was a duplicate of the P.S. *Glen Avon*.

Assassination

These halcyon days were soon shattered by the reported assassination of the Archduke Franz Ferdinand and his wife, the Duchess of Hohenburg, by a 19 year old student Gavrilo Princip as the imperial car crossed a small hump-backed bridge in Sarajevo on 28 June. The wars his action precipitated were to take a hundred million lives in one way or another and effectively created the modern world. Britain declared war on Germany on 4 August and the *West Somerset Free Press* carried the headline ***THE GREAT WAR.***

The first paddle steamers to be 'called up' from any fleet from the UK were Campbell's *Devonia* and *Brighton Queen*. They left Bristol for Devonport on 30 Sept to be fitted out for minesweeping duties.

Tall Tale

The pier once figured in an intriguing story linked with Germany and the 1914-18 war. It was rumoured that Kaiser Wilhelm II himself had landed in disguise from a steamer at Minehead pier. He had been driven away by car to Croydon Hall to a secret meeting with Count Conrad Hockburg, the German owner of the Hall, where activities were increasingly coming under suspicion. The sequel, when war eventually broke out between Britain and Germany, was a tremendous spy scare with Croydon Hall as the focal point. Count Hockburg, sensing the imminence of war, left Croydon Hall on 28 July and England on 3 August to volunteer for service in Germany with the Red Cross. The Crown seized the Hall and contents, that much was fact.

Casualties

Sadly, Campbell's paddle steamers *Brighton* Queen and *Lady Ismay* were sunk by mines in October and December 1915 respectively.

In 1916, my father Stanley was conscripted into the Army and served with the Somerset Light Infantry. Whilst in Palestine he was wounded at Nablus and was carried to a field dressing station over the shoulder of another local man, Fred Winter an ex-pit farrier from the Rhondda whose family had earlier crossed the Bristol Channel from South Wales and settled in Minehead, as did many others.

Another interesting sideshow happened on 11 March 1916 when the P.S. *Westward Ho!* and P.S. *Glen Avon* were deployed on salvaging the Zeppelin L15 which had been brought down by anti-aircraft fire at the entrance to the Thames estuary.

24 - P.S. Brighton Queen

25 - P.S. Lady Ismay

P.S. Glen Avon.

26 - P.S. Glen Avon. Built 1912 by the Ailsa Shipbuilding Company, Troon.

27 - P.S. Duchess of Devonshire

Built 1892 for the Devon Steamship Company. During the summers of 1917 and 1918, a solitary white funnelled steamer plied the waters of the Bristol Channel. She was the small paddle steamer *Duchess of Devonshire* on charter from the Devon Dock, Pier & Steamship Company Ltd. Of Exmouth, and maintained the Campbell's Cardiff to Weston ferry.

Close Call

On the 15 June 1918, the *West Somerset Free Press* reported a floating mine had been washed ashore at Gore Point Porlock and a minesweeper arrived to explode it.

Armistice and Survival

The Great War ended with the Armistice being signed on 11 November 1918. Surviving steamers of the White Funnel Fleet were retained by the Admiralty for use in a post-war mine clearance scheme. Because of the uncertainty of the availability of vessels, the services of the P.S. *Duchess of Devonshire* were retained and she opened the 1919 season on 4 June. She completed her charter at the end of September and returned to Exmouth on 4 October. The *Duchess* cruised the Channel toward Minehead for three hours on 17 and 19 July – fare 2s.

Competition

In March 1919 two Campbell's steamers, the P.S. *Albion* and P.S. *Ravenswood* returned home to Bristol after war service. On 12 July Campbell's White Funnel steamers resumed their pleasure sailings after an absence of five years. Trips from Minehead to Ilfracombe and Clovelly were advertised. Competition arrived in the shape of Tuckers of Cardiff Yellow Funnel Fleet – P.S. *Lady Moyra* and P.S. *Lady Evelyn* and so the rivalry began.

Racing generally took place on the Ilfracombe route. On Wednesday, 16 July the P.S. *Glen Avon* reached Minehead first and P.S. *Lady Moyra* was ten minutes behind her when she left Minehead pier but overhauled the White Funnel steamer and arrived two minutes ahead at Ilfracombe. On Monday, 11 August, two old adversaries from pre-war days competed. The P.S. *Lady Moyra* was scheduled to sail to Ilfracombe via Minehead, but this call was omitted when it was learned the P. S. *Cambria* was going direct. Little regard being paid to the passengers waiting on Minehead pier.

P. & A. Campbell's, Bristol Channel Passenger Steamers.
ON BOARD P.S. "ALBION".

28 - P.S. Albion arriving at Ilfracombe

29 - P.S. Ravenswood

P.S. Cambria.

30 - P.S. Cambria. Built 1895. Known as the 'Greyhound of the South'

P.S. BRITANNIA

31 - P.S. Britannia

Throughout 1919, industrial unrest began to grow, culminating with a National Rail Strike starting on Saturday 27 September, eventually forcing 600,000 people out of work. The coal supply situation brought about a serious reduction of the services of both steamer fleets but Campbell's, who held a larger coal reserve, were able to carry on and survive the nine days of the strike.

CHAPTER FOUR

The Twenties

At the 20th ordinary Annual General Meeting of the shareholders of the Minehead Pier Company on 31 January 1920, a profit of £155 was shown on the year's working. The winter had been very mild and there were signs of an abnormally early spring. The *West Somerset Free Press* of 7 February reported a Miss Vellacott having picked ripe whortle-berries (blueberries) on North Hill.

Whit Monday, 24 May Bristol Channel pleasure sailings started rather earlier than usual. Boats of both the White Funnel and Yellow Funnel fleets made frequent calls at Minehead pier en-route from Cardiff to Ilfracombe.

On 29 May, the death was announced of Mr Clement Kille who gave up the headmastership of Old Cleeve School to join the *Free Press* as a journalist. He was, as mentioned earlier, the Secretary of the Minehead Improvement & Publicity Association. He was also a very keen photographer and a picture of the pier taken by him earlier in the year is shown below.

32 - Photograph taken from the top of a gasometer shows the pier's superstructure c1920

33 - A View across the bay of the pier and steamer leaving for Ilfracombe c1920

Another unhappy event occurred on 7 August when Captain Edward John Perkins aged 71, the Minehead Piermaster collapsed and died on the pier as he waited the arrival of the P.S. Britannia. At one time Captain Perkins was the owner of vessels trading out of Minehead.

Two further pictures of the pier c1920 were taken by John Valentine & Son, the well-known postcard producers of London and Dundee.

34 - Quay from North Hill c1920 by J. Valentine

Two views of the entrance to the pier by John Valentine c1920. Top, also shows the old stone jetty and, in the distance, Warren Point (where Butlin's holiday camp now stands).

35 - Harbour from North Hill by J. Valentine

Below, a similar view with a closer look at the busy harbour and the Pier Hotel in the foreground.

Deep Water

The end of the pier was 700 feet from land. Time came when the Pier Company as well as the pier were in 'deep water'. An extraordinary meeting of the Company was held on Tuesday 5 July to consider its financial position. There had been virtually no income during the 1914-18 war (the pier formerly yielded an annual gross income of approximately £700) and repairs had become necessary, especially to the landing stages. On top of this there was a coal strike and a further loss of revenue. After discussion it was decided to go into voluntary liquidation and the Chairman stated that arrangements would be put in hand for the pier to be sold at auction.

The *West Somerset Free Press* of 23 July later reported 'Minehead's 20 year old pier was duly offered for sale by auction by Messres James Phillips & Sons at the Plume of Feathers Hotel on Friday 22 July 1921. After brisk bidding it was knocked down Mr R Tucker of Messrs W H Tucker & Co Ltd of Cardiff, the owners of the Yellow Funnel Steamboat line'. An amenity which had cost £12,000 now went for the purchase price of £2,550.

Plume of Feathers Hotel, Minehead, Somerset.

36 - The Plume of Feathers Hotel c1908. The Model T Ford has the street to itself.

The Tide Turns

At Campbell's board meeting in October 1921 it was reported that Tucker's had failed to complete their recent purchase of Minehead pier. Campbell's solicitors had therefore re-opened negotiations and it was proposed and seconded that they should purchase the pier. The board also heard Captain Peter Campbell's report on his meeting with Ernest Tucker at which he was informed that Tucker's were prepared to sell the P.S. *Lady Moyra* and the P.S. *Lady Evelyn* for £50,000.

On Thursday 27 October a meeting of the creditors of the Yellow Funnel Fleet took place at the Imperial Hotel, Cardiff, and the Company went into liquidation. The opposition was over. It appeared that Campbell's did not really want to buy the two 'ladies' *Moyra* and *Evelyn*, but the purchase price of £24,498 for the pair was too tempting, after all they could re-sell at a profit later on, but this never happened.

An Ill Wind

On 3 September the *West Somerset Free Press* reported that something had gone wrong with the weather vane on Minehead pier. A correspondent had written to say 'the Welsh coast stood on the South side of the Channel, the sun was rising in the West, the mouth of the Channel was due East and Exmoor guarded Minehead on the North!'

5 March 1921 the newspaper reported that the P.S. *Waverley* and P.S. *Glen Rosa* two popular Bristol Channel pleasure steamers of Campbell's White Funnel Fleet were up for sale. Twenty years before they were regarded as the last word in pleasure steamers.

Improvements To The Pier

Early in 1922, the new owners, Campbell's, began making alterations and improvements to the pier and by the beginning of June had spent thousands of pounds preparing for the new season and it was now considered a credit to the town. Another busy season of steamer calling was in prospect.

37 - Steamers seen arriving and leaving the pier c1922

The hunting season attracted hundreds of additional visitors and the Minehead herrings were running well. There was such a glut they were hard to sell even at a penny each at the door.

38 - Dunster lawns polo ground

In May 1923 the 100th Yeomanry Brigade was camped on North Hill when the Commanding Officer of the 399th Oxford Yeomanry Battery, Major, the Rt Hon, Winston Churchill paid a visit and took part in a polo match on Dunster Lawns.

P.S. "GLEN GOWER"

P. & A. CAMPBELL, LTD.

39 - P.S. Glen Gower c 1922

On Thursday, 7 June the P.S. *Glen Gower*, (built in 1922 by the Ailsa Shipbuilding Co, Troon) made a record crossing of the Bristol Channel from the Mumbles, Swansea to Ilfracombe in just one hour and sixteen minutes. How long would it take us now to travel between the same two points?

The August Bank Holiday was one of the most crowded Minehead had ever known. On Monday 1,500 people arrived by train, 600 by steamers and an incalculable number by car and coach. The pier had a record day – 1,500 people getting on and off.

During late September, stormy weather once again caused widespread disruption to sailings. On Thursday 20th P.S. *Westward Ho!* an hour out of Barry en-route to Ilfracombe struck a heavy sea and a float broke away. Off Culver Sands she met the P.S. Barry on her way from Cardiff to Minehead where she landed her 226 passengers and then took the 79 passengers off the *Westward Ho!* and towed her to Sully Island.

40 - P.S. Barry at Watchet in her Barry Railway colours (red funnel) c1907

Sailing on the Sabbath

An innovation of the 1924 season was Sunday sailings in the Bristol Channel. Although the White Funnel steamers had run regularly on Sundays on the South Coast it just was not done in the Bristol Channel! The first Sunday passenger carrying sailing was an afternoon cruise along the Gower Coast from Swansea by the P.S. *Glen Gower* on 29 June. Gradually Sunday sailings to Ilfracombe were accepted.

41 - A photograph of the P.S. Devonia leaving Minehead pier c1924

Tug of War

An article in the *West Somerset Free Press* of 14 June 1924 described the scene of such a contest as had never been witnessed before. On the breezy summit of Dunkery Beacon (1,704 ft) a party belonging to the Powell Duffryn Steam Coal Company had held a tug of war there. The visitors had come over to Minehead on a White Funnel steamer for the day.

42 - Motor cyclists en-route to Lynton c1924

This photograph taken on the 11th July 1924 shows two motorcycle passengers resting by Minehead pier en-route to Lynton. Everything on board, 'plus the kitchen sink'.

In early September one of the largest sharks seen on the south side of the Bristol Channel was caught in the fishing nets of Mr John Slade of Quay Street, Minehead. The bottle-nosed specimen measuring 6 feet 6½ inches was put on show. Late November a round-headed porpoise or 'caacing' whale was stranded on the beach near Swill Point, Donniford.

The weather during the summer of 1925 showed an improvement over the previous years, however, it was not without mishaps. The P.S. *Glen Avon* ran into difficulties on 15th May during an afternoon trip from Weston to Minehead. Around teatime, a heavy sea-fog rolled in and after the steamer had left Minehead pier it became denser: unable to see, at 9 pm she grounded off Brean Down. She eventually floated off and reached Cardiff at 10 pm.

The year ended with some good news, the local squire, Mr Luttrell, had offered Minehead Urban District Council the foreshore on a 999 year lease.

Exmoor had a white Christmas and the snow lay very deep. On New Year's Day 1926, twelve hours of continuous rain produced bad flooding in West Somerset.

All Change

On Monday 12 July 270 passengers boarded the pleasure steamer Cambria at the pier for a trip to Ilfracombe. The steamer with approximately 850 passengers aboard ran onto rocks at Rillage Point in dense fog. All the passengers were safely taken off but it was the P.S. Glen Usk (who had stood by during the grounding) who brought them home again. At the end of July, the *West Somerset Free Press* reported that thousands of jelly fish were washed up on Minehead beach, also that Minehead had a summer population of 15,000.

Welsh 'Choirs'

The Sunday sailings to Ilfracombe had become very popular. Local residents and visitors would climb the zig-zag walk on North Hill overlooking the pier and jetty to watch the steamers leaving for South Wakes and listen to the Welsh passengers singing hymns especially 'Cwm Rhondda' as the boats sailed into the darkness of the Channel. Such a scene can be conjured up in the illustration below.

The Pier, Minehead

43 - The Paddle Steamer Glen Usk arriving at Minehead Pier at sunset on a summer evening c1926

Early in April 1927, the largest vessel to ever enter Minehead harbour was the steamer Eleth (400 tons). It berthed with 390 tons of cracked stones for the Urban District Council.

In November Minehead's old lifeboat, the George Lester was sent away BY RAIL to its new owner, a man in North Wales.

Messrs. P & A Campbell announced a profit of £16,966 for the year.

The 1928 season opened at Easter and it was so cold, snow fell the following week but preceded a reasonably good summer. Sadly, on 10 December Captain Alec Campell died at his home at Ferngrove, in Kilmun, aged 66. He and his brother Peter were joint owners of the White Funnel Fleet and since 1921 were the sole operators of excursion steamers in the Bristol Channel. On the first trip to Ilfracombe in 1929 the P.S. Glen Usk flew her flags at half mast as a mark of respect.

44 - Captain Alec Campbell (from the Chris Collard Collection)

The atmosphere of the time is summed up by Chris Collard in his book *White Funnels* Volume 2. With the 1929 season over, the decade drew to its close. In retrospect the years since the Great War had not been easy. The Company was so dependent on the weather and in the past eleven seasons, only four had produced what could be termed ' good' summers in terms of passenger figures. In addition, the coal strikes, the General Strike and rising unemployment all conspired to inflict further damage to the Company's operation. October 1929 had brought the Wall Street crash, and, although far from home, the predicament of the American economy was to have repercussions throughout the whole of western Europe. However, the British people, with their customary resiliance and their capacity for 'making the most of it', rose above the gloom and despondency in their determination to enjoy themselves.

45 - Pier from the 'Zig Zag' walks 1929. P.S. Glen Gower just departing

CHAPTER FIVE

The Years Leading To World War Two

Following the death of Alec Campbell, Captain Peter was joined by his new associate Mr W J Banks, who had joined the Board of Directors in May 1926. Despite bad weather from July to September the Company showed a profit of £4,463 with an available balance of £7,247.

THE PIER, MINEHEAD   11768

46 - 1930 P.S. Ravenswood at the Pier viewed from the Zig Zag walk on North Hill

This picture illustrates an idyllic picture of the pier, a calm sea and the P.S. *Ravenswood* calling at the lower level

The 1931 season was described as the 'most abysmal of the decade'. It was one of the worst years of the depression and the summer weather was atrocious. On Saturday, 28 March a Greek ship the *Taxiachis* loaded with 4,000 tones of coal was driven ashore on Lundy and remained there for two years following a south east gale. Several steamers visited Minehead during the season. Sunday 5 July P.S. *Lady Moyra* after visiting the battleship *Malaya*, Monday, 10 August P.S. Britannia on her way to Padstow and, on Sunday 16 August, P.S. *Glen Gower* called en-route from Ilfracombe.

On Bank Holiday Monday 3 August there was a fire on Penarth pier.

On Sunday 16 August, to crown it all, gales swept across the southern half of the counrtry. At Minehead the tide was so high that the top platform of the pier was awash so the P.S. *Glen Gower* had to put into the old stone jetty to pick up passengers. Not all those who had disembarked in the morning could make the jetty owing to the flooding of the promenade by the abnormal tide. The overall effects of this disastrous season were reflected in the White Funnel Fleet accounts which showed a net loss of £2, 686.

P.S. Brighton Belle

47 - The P.S. Brighton Belle ex Lady Evelyn made its first run in the Bristol Channel on Friday 13 May 1932.

Leaving Exmouth

48 - P.S. Duke of Devonshire seen leaving Exmouth, joined the Campbell's fleet in 1933, the year china whistles were fitted to most of Campbell's steamers

On Tuesday 18 July after an evening trip to Minehead, 100 passengers spent the night in the Channel when the *Glen Avon* ran aground in thick fog near Rhoose in South Wales.

Fortunes appeared to have turned and the Company returned profits of £12,770 and £14, 104 in 1932/3 seasons respectively.

49 - Honeymoon 30s Style

In June 1934 my parents, Stanley and Elizabeth were married. They made their vows to each other in the morning, then boarded the *Devonia* and sailed down to Ilfracombe. They sat on Capstone Hill and enjoyed a picnic prepared earlier (Honeymoons' in Barbados, Thailand or Tenerife were unheard of in those days) – then sailed home again in the evening.

50 - Capstone Hill, Ilfracombe – with a steamer just leaving

In 1935, the highlight of the season was the Silver Jubilee Royal Naval Review at Spithead on 16 July. At least four of the White Funnel Fleet were present including the P.S. *Glen Gower.*

51 - The Glen Gower seen leaving Minehead Pier c1935 (Photo by Francis Frith)

On Saturday, 27 June P.S. *Ravenswood* sustained damage to a paddle on an evening trip to Ilfracombe from Newport at Hurlstone Point.

31 December Captain Peter Campbell retired.

The 'Feel Good' Factor

1936 was the year the United Kingdom had three monarchs (just), King George V, Edward VIII and King George VI. The British economy was improving, unemployment was coming down and as far as Minehead was concerned, the seaside resort was full. It was a year that would see many changes. In May the RMS *Queen Mary* sailed on her maiden voyage to New York and the P.S. *Gracie Fields* was launched in Southampton. In June Gatwick airport came into operation and in July the Spanish Civil War broke out. The BBC launched the worlds first scheduled T.V. service and Jessie Owen, a black American athlete won four gold medals at the Berlin Olympics. In October the famous Jarrow march began and President Roosevelt was selected for a second term of office. Crystal Palace caught fire and to crown it all, Rudyard Kipling died of a burst duodenal ulcer.

Minehead Swimming Pool, taken from the air.

52 - Minehead swimming pool c1936

Minehead's heated sea-water bathing pool opened on Saturday 13th of June 1936 with the National Championships. Built to Olympic specifications it was where Helen Barton (diver) and Paul Radmilovic (swimmer) trained regularly. Paul competed in six Olympic Games and captained the British team three times. Many of his cups and trophies could be seen in the foyer of the old "Plume of Feathers" hotel, sad to say, both the pool and the hotel were demolished.

My father Stanley helped to build the pool and when I was born he was thrown into the pool by his workmates to celebrate my arrival. He always maintained he was the first person to swim in the pool!

53 – Minehead swimming pool entrance

54 - P.S. Cambria at Minehead Pier en-route for Ilfracombe c 1936 (Chris Collard Collection)

Coronation

On 12 May 1937 the coronation of King George VI and Queen Elizabeth took place at Westminster Abbey. There was another Royal Naval Review at Spithead on 20 May, where no less than seven White Funnel steamers were present, these were P.S. *Waverley, Glen Gower, Brighton Queen, Britannia, Cambria, Glen Usk and Devonia.*

Local Amenity

Any seaside resort of note felt it needed a pier to enhance its status, Minehead was no exception. Although it was built for somewhere boats could call, it was strictly functional, no entertainments provided, but holidaymakers and locals enjoyed a stroll along its length. The inter-war years were arguably the 'golden age' for piers, with people wishing to put the horrors of conflict behind them.

55 - Rosie and Alice Rawle with Minnie Stenner (centre) strolling along Minehead pier c1937. Photo by Martin Cross ARPS

Somewhere the Moon Doesn't Shine

The *West Somerset Free Press* recalled a true story which happened in 1937. On a summer's evening, the P.S. Westward Ho!, called at Minehead pier on her way from Ilfracombe to Cardiff. A sunburnt, slightly sozzled son of the Somerset soil staggered aboard the steamer, looked up at the moon, proceeded to wave to it and waxed valedictory. "Goodbye, ol' mewn, goodbye. I shall never zee 'ee again, so I shan't, cos I be gwain auver to Cardiff to work".

56 - Jack and Marjorie Rawle off to catch the steamer to Cardiff c1937. Photo by Marin Cross Bluebird Studios. The Avenue.

The 1937 season finished once again showing handsome profit for Campbell's of £26,885.

The Beginning of the End

On Sunday 18 December 1938 Captain Peter Campbell died at his home in Wooton-Under-Edge. He was 80. He was regarded as one of the finest seamen who ever stepped aboard a paddle steamer. A freemason and a man of considerable generosity.

57 - Captain Peter Campbell (CCC)

58 - Captain Peter Campbell's grave at Wotton-under-Edge c1954 (Chris Collard Collection).

The Pier, Minehead

59 - Glen Gower 1938

Copyright
Mnd. 38

ARRIVAL OF STEAMER. - MINEHEAD.

Raphael Tuck
& Sons, Ltd.

60 - Glen Gower 1938

61 - P.S. Cambria arriving at Minehead Pier 1938/1939 (H.G. Owen)

The Ides of March

The 1939 season opened on a note of optimism after the signing of the Munich Pact in September 1938. However, the political situation in Europe was deteriorating until, in March, German troops marched into Prague. The season continued without incident until the end of August. On 1 September Germany advanced into Poland and two days later Britain was at war again. For Campbell's White Funnel fleet it marked the end of another era and for the second time in its history the Company prepared for conflict. All eleven steamers were commandeered by the Admiralty and were quickly converted for minesweeping duties.

62 - P.S. Ravenswood arriving at Minehead Pier 1938/1939

This photo by A. F. Sergeant for F Frith & Co shows P.S. Ravenswood arriving at Minehead pier for the last time – August 1939. A visitor (or local resident) sitting on the breakwater pondering the future. This was probably one of the last pictures ever taken of the pier before it was dismantled.

62 R.S. *Ravenswood* drawing at Morehead pier 1906-1909

This poster by A. E. Seagrim for F. Potts & Co shows *R.S. Ravenswood* arriving at Morehead pier for the last time. A gust of wind broke her hull and sank her the breakwater pondering the future. This was probably one of the last pictures ever taken of her name it was manufactured.

CHAPTER SIX

1940 The Pier Must Go

On instructions from the War Office, Minehead was ordered to sacrifice the pier to allow search lights and two four inch guns mounted on the old harbour, an uninterrupted field of fire down Channel. Although there were a dozen or so other piers along the Bristol Channel coastline, and even more facing France on the South coast, Minehead's pier was the only one to be completely dismantled and never replaced.

Messrs P & A Campbell, the owners of the pier since 1921, were paid £90,000 in compensation, but rather than spending the money on a replacement once the war was over, it was used to improve their steamer fleet.

The pier's ironwork was taken across the channel to South Wales for salvage, but after the conflict was still lying rusting in the mud at Newport. Some timber from the pier's decking was used to build a farm extension near Exford. The remainder (I have on good authority) provided a few locals with firewood for a very long time.

A Fine Craftsman

Appropriately named Noah Boatfield of Kingsbrompton, was a smith renowned for his ironwork and its ornamentation. He was also engaged on the ironwork in the construction of the pier in 1900, never dreaming that the structure would one day have to be demolished as a safeguard against enemy invasion. His craft is said to stand very high in the eyes of Minehead residents, none higher than the vane on top of St. Michael's Church tower. What remains of the pier head and entrance ramp is now owned by a local fisherman.

The demolition work was completed by May 1940, by which time there were further observations from the gunners that they feared the recoil and detonation were affecting the foundations of the harbour and the platform was not sufficiently strong. By the time this information had filtered through to the War Office department responsible for local coastal defences, it had become clear that the proposed invasion of the United Kingdom was no longer at the top of Hitler's list, and an order was posted to remove the gun.

63 - View from the North Hill, Minehead taken in September 1940 of the dismantling of the pier. (From the Ken Jenkins collection)

64 - All that remains of the pier today (2004). Aberthaw can clearly be seen across on the South Wales coastline.

Post-Mortem

Most of us now know, that had we not won the Battle of Britain in September 1940, 'Operation Sealion' would have gone ahead,. 'Under Directive No 16' Hitler planned to invade and occupy England. A landing at Lyme Regis would have launched his sixth army northwards, through Somerset, and establish a headquarters in Bristol.

In the Autumn of 1940, a local lady stopped to give a soldier a lift somewhere along the old A38. The wayside soldier was dressed in British khaki, wearing a great coat with a rifle slung over his shoulder. He spoke the most incoherent English ever heard and said he wished to go to Bristol. The lady dropped him off at the Tramway Centre. To this day she is convinced he was a German paratrooper.

Another rumour at the time was of a German invasion by way of Ireland. This would have involved a sea and air attack up the Bristol Channel.

An article in the *West Somerset Free Press* 26 September 1940 reported 'two large-scale attacks on Filton airfield and the Bristol Aircraft Company works. 170 enemy aircraft came up the Bristol Channel and a widespread running fight ensued. The air over Somerset was hot with combat.'

These threats were taken seriously and a series of defences (pillboxes and obstacles) were built in a line from the river Parrett estuary to Seaton on the mouth of the river Axe. This became known as the 'Inter-Channel STOP line'.

CHAPTER SEVEN

Hope For The Future

There have been several attempts to replace the pier but so far without success. The first came in September 1946 when plans were made to rebuild the pier with government funding, estimated to be in the region of £70,000, but because of the shortage of steel, the government withdrew its support. The Urban District Council discussed the possibility of having a reinforced concrete pier in the same position as the one taken down in September 1940, but were unable to finance such an undertaking. As a compromise it would arrange for the accumulation of shingle obstructing the entrance to the harbour, known locally as 'the patch' to be dredged to allow sufficient depth for steamers to call again.

On Whit Monday, 6 June 1949 Campbell's latest paddle steamer *Cardiff Queen* called off Lynmouth for the first time since 1939. Forty passengers were landed by launches

On Saturday, 2 June 1951, almost fifty years after Mr George Fownes Luttrell had opened the pier, Mr Geoffrey Luttrell handed over the harbour, his ancestor George Luttrell had had build in 1612, to the Town. It was sold to the UDC. for £2 on the understanding that the surrounding land should not be used for a lunatic asylum, a hospital or a public house and on his death, for a further £150, the foreshore was also sold.

The opening ceremony was performed by Vice-Admiral P.K. Knight, Admiral Superintendent at Devonport and thousands watched the arrival of the P.S. *Glen Usk*, the first pleasure steamer to call at Minehead since August 1939. Mr Geoffrey Luttrell, Lord of the Manor, handed over the deeds of the harbour to the Chairman of Minehead UDC, Mr William Webber, together with a painting of the harbour which had hung in Dunster Castle for over 300 years. The Chairman's daughter Miss Joyce Webber presented a bouquet of flowers to the Mayoress of Cardiff. Seven Somerset mayors also attended the ceremony. As in 1901, following the opening of the pier, a civic reception took place in the Hotel Metropole. Afterwards, invited guests and dignitaries went for a cruise on the steamer down as far as Porlock Bay.

In September 1956, on the same day the P.S. Britannia made her last voyage. The death occurred of one of the vessels oldest and most frequent passengers, Mr Harold Lailey, he had rarely missed an opportunity to make any of the longer voyages out of Minehead. During the war, Mr Lailey was an Air Raid Warden for Periton.

66 - P.S. Glen Usk entering Minehead harbour, 2 June 1951. The ketch Emma Louise, moved to make room for her berthing

65 - Mr Geoffrey Luttrell handing over the deeds and painting of Minehead harbour to Mr William Webber, Chairman of the UDC on 2 June 1951

66 - P.S. Glen Usk entering Minehead harbour 2 June 1951. The ketch Emma Louise moved to make room for her berthing

67 - P & A Campbell's White funnel steamers called regularly during the 1950s including P.S. Ravenswood and P.S. Britannia

68 - P.S. Ravenswood entering Minehead harbour in the early 1950s. Photo by Blackmore of Minehead

On Saturday, 28 September 1957, P.S. *Glen Gower* on a return trip from Barry to Ilfracombe, took one and a half hours to cross to Minehead and eventually arrived in Ilfracombe on Sunday morning. For most of the trip the boiler pressure was only half what it should have been. She returned to Penarth never to sail again under her own steam.

July 1961 – Tom Rawle of the Cabin Café Quay Street was out in his motor boat and rescued five language students working as domestics in the "Plume of Feathers" hotel who were cut off by the tide.

Butlin's Holiday Camp

Billy Butlin opened his holiday camp at Minehead in May 1962 for 18 weeks only and attracted 35,000 full-board campers plus 50,000 day visitors. A year later the development allowed the capacity to increase to 10,500 and the camp opened for Christmas for the first time. This not only boosted Minehead's economy, but provided a source of revenue on Saturdays for Campbell's (now part of the George Nott Organisation) steamer trade. Through bookings were available from Barry and Cardiff to Weston-Super-Mare, thence by coach to Minehead and vice versa. The word 'camp' was dropped in favour of holiday centre under the ownership of Bourne Leisure which is the parent company of Butlin's Holiday World.

70 - An early view of Butlin's Camp taken from the North Hill Minehead by R Blackmore. The old swimming pool can be seen to the right of the camp

Cruising and Queens

Nowadays these two words have different connotations but in the 1960s in the Bristol Channel cruising meant a boat trip down to Ilfracombe and Lundy Island on a White funnel paddle steamer. The 'Queens' were Campbell's two latest vessels, the *Bristol Queen* and *Cardiff Queen*, launched since the war. The 1965-6 seasons were disastrous for the company. On Thursday9 September 1965, the P.S. *Cardiff Queen* was out of service at Barry with radius rod trouble. The *Bristol Queen* was similarly disabled off Mineheadwhile returning from Ilfracombe and a replacement rod having to be fitted overnight at Barry.

On Friday, 24 September P.S. *Bristol Queen* left Minehead harbour on the high tide, on her return from Ilfracombe to Barry and Cardiff, she damaged her starboard paddle when it scraped along the harbour wall as the sponson mounted a 'guard beam' and had to return to Cardiff at half speed.

In 1966 the two 'Queens' handled most of the down channel sailings while the M.V. (Motor Vessel) *Westward Ho* maintained the ferry and up channel services. She did however make her first call to Minehead on Saturday 18 June. On Friday, 19 August the M.V. *Westward Ho* made a trip to Minehead. Many of the passengers were from the one hundred and twenty on the P.S. *Bristol Queen* which had hit and damaged Penarth pier.

Another visitor to Minehead was the M.V. *St Trillo* (ex *St Silio*) with 290 passengers on board on the 1st May 1965.

71 - The P.S. Bristol Queen at Minehead harbour 1966

72 - P.S. Cardiff Queen arriving at Ilfracombe

73 - M.V. Westward Ho (ex Victa) seen leaving Porthcawl. Operated by P & A Campbell's on Bristol Channel 1965-1971

74 - M.V. St Trillo. Built in 1936 as St Silio for the North Wales service. Re-named St Trillo in 1945. Operated by P & A Campbell's on the Bristol Channel from 1963-1969

Ancient Monuments

In November 1977 a series of large stone fish traps (or weirs) off Minehead Harbour, which date back to the 13th century, were scheduled as Ancient Monuments by the Department for the Environment. They are still in use.

75 - This photo by Christopher Jones shows the Medieval Fish Weirs still in use in Minehead today

Campbell's Last Trip

Another attempt to rebuild the pier happened in 1978 when architects, Peter and Sue Barker, who lived on the North Hill Minehead planned to build a new £500,000 pier. The Victorian style development would have had old style amusements and attractions on it; they felt this was just what Minehead needed to brighten up the sea-front. It was a brave idea, but the timing was bad, so it failed. Passenger numbers declined consistently and Campbell's finally decided to call it a day and stopped running trips from Minehead in 1979. They ran a single season in 1980 for the Landmark Trust.

CHAPTER EIGHT

Prince Ivanhoe To The Rescue

An effort was made in 1981 to revive the Bristol Channel sailings, when the ex 'sealink' ferry *Shanklin* from the Portsmouth to Ryde (where the first British pier was built in 1814) service, was purchased by a group of enthusiasts. This Motor Vessel was operated by the Firth of Clyde Steam Packet Company on their behalf, with the intention that any profits should be allocated to help towards the operational preservation of the P.S. *Waverley* an ex Clyde vessel which had become the world" last sea-going paddle steamer.

Shanklin was re-named *Prince Ivanhoe* and, working in conjunction with *Waverley*, she was placed on some of the old Campbell routes in the Bristol Channel. Whilst on a cruise off the Gower coast in August 1971 she struck an underwater obstruction in Port Eynon Bay, had to be beached and became a total loss.

76 - Prince Ivanhoe ex Shanklin at City Docks, Bristol

77 - Prince Ivanhoe

Following the loss of the *Prince Ivanhoe* a new partner was found in 1986. Although in a deplorable state, the M.V. *Balmoral* was restored at a cost of £500,000 and joined the fleet run by the Paddle Steamer Preservation Society.

78 - The P.S. Waverley calling in at Minehead

The *Waverley* is mainly employed in Scottish waters during the summer, but undertakes occasional tours in English waters at the beginning and end of each season in an attempt to provide coastal excursions from the piers and ports which otherwise would be completely devoid of the sound and sight of a traditional excursion steamer. Both the P.S. *Waverley* and M.V. *Balmoral* make regular visits to Minehead each season and long may they continue to do so.

79 - M.V. Balmoral in Minehead Harbour

Integrated Transport System

An ambitious venture was offered by Hoverwest Ltd in 1985 involving travel by hovercraft, paddle steamers and steam train. The public and holidaymakers would be offered a 'package deal' whereby only one ticket was necessary. A daily hovercraft service between Minehead and Barry would begin on 23 May. It would coincide with sailings of the *Waverley* paddle steamer from Portishead, Avonmouth, Minehead, Barry, Penarth and Newport from May 24 to June 26. The West Somerset Railway would, as usual be running steam trains to Bishops Lydeard throughout the summer. The scheme failed, would you believe it, through lack of passengers!

80 - Hovercraft

Minehead – South Wales Ferry

Ten years later in April 1995 the Bristol Channel high-speed passenger ferry network was proposed linking Minehead with South Wales. There would be six key ports, Minehead, Ilfracombe, Weston, Swansea, Barry and Cardiff. In March 1996 top engineers gave the green light for plans to build a new £5 million pier in Minehead for the start of the new millennium. Permission would have had to be granted directly by the government under a complicated statutory order which could take up to two years to finalise. There was overwhelming support by County and District Councils who were looking at possible schemes which could qualify for European Objective 5b funding. Support for plans to rebuild the pier came from Waverley Excursions Ltd who considered a pier at Minehead to be pivotal to their future Bristol Channel services, especially as the piers at Penarth and Clevedon had received substantial renovation grants of £6.5m.

Minehead Sea Defences Scheme

In the Autumn of 1996 the tail end of *Hurricane Lily* devastated the sea front, the West Somerset Railway, Butlins and the Golf Club were badly flooded. Work on the revamped sea-defences scheme costing approximately £13m was underway and would take four years to complete.

Minehead Pier 2000 Association had until July to meet the deadline for submitting its funding bid to the Millennium Commission for the first traditional pier to be built in Britain for almost a century.

81 - An artist's impression of how the pier could look

Six months later in January 1997 informal plans showing a possible £5 million space-age pier for Minehead was put on display in a series of exhibitions across West Somerset. The new proposal was to use state of the art technology and materisl to create a sweeping curve of a a pier to mirror the harbour and reflect seafaring traditions of the town.

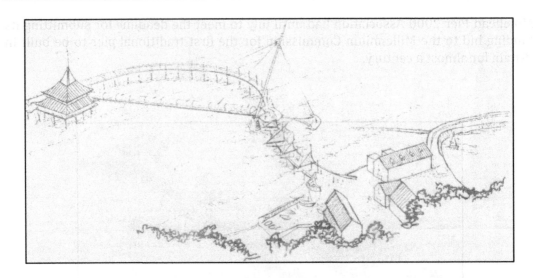

82 - The architect's sketch of what Minehead's pier of the future could look like

An eleventh hour intervention by the world famous science fiction author Arthur C Clarke, a Freeman of Minehead, proved not enough to save the town's proposal. The Millennium Pier was missing from the Commission's final list of 71 projects on which to spend £221 million.

It appeared that the European money did not materialise because £5 million had been given to the Eden project to provide botanical gardens near St Austell in Cornwall.

'Yes' Minister

The tourism Minister Janet Anderson, told councilors on her visit to Minehead in July 2000 to re-submit their lottery application for a new pier which would include a fast catamaran service to South Wales. The previous bid had failed because there was not enough money left in the pot.

83 - Tourism Minister Janet Anderson with Colin Hill at Minehead

In November the town's Chamber of Trade resurrected plans to build a £6 million pier at Minehead. They felt a replacement pier was vital to the region's tourist industry and would offer healthy returns to any private investor.

Most people wanted to see a traditional pier built rather than one featuring futuristic elements as proposed in 1996/7. The Millennium Commission asked the Pier Association to change the pier plans, which they did, and then refused to give them any money.

84 - Locals wanted to see an ordinary traditional replacement pier in the town similar to that illustrated here

Centenary of the Pier and Golden Anniversary of the Harbour

On Friday, 25 May 2001, the anniversary of the opening of Minehead pier was remembered by a display of cards and photographs, by kind permission of George Oyston and staff, at the General Computer & Office Services in Friday Street, Minehead. A planned visit by the Paddle Steamer Preservation Society of the P.S. *Waverley* was, unfortunately, cancelled. However, on Friday 20 July the *Balmoral* sailed into the harbour for a delayed celebration to mark the 100th anniversary of the town's pier and the 50th anniversary of the harbour opening. Mr Stan Taylor, Chairman of West Somerset District Council and Meigan Lyons, Chairman of the Minehead Town Council welcomed the *Balmoral* and they enjoyed a special cruise on her down to Porlock Bay.

The event was marked with a presentation by Mike Telstone, the publicity officer of the Bristol Channel branch of the Paddle Steamer Preservation Society of a framed picture of the *Balmoral's* sister ship *Waverley*, built in 1886, alongside Minehead harbour. Councillor Taylor said he hoped the picture would be displayed in the District Council chamber as a lasting memento of the link between Minehead and the pleasure steamers *Waverley* and *Balmoral*.

On the 1st of June, local boatman Alan Keirle launched *Ark Supreme* after four years of being told his dream boat was 8½ inches too long for the harbour.

85 - July 2001. Presentation by Mike Telstone PSPS to the Chairman (Stan Taylor) Minehead UDC to celebrate the opening of the pier on 25 May 1901. Also pictured – Cllr Meigan Lyons, Moyra Denby (PSPS) and Captain Edward Davies of the Balmoral

That Sinking Feeling

In January 2003 a fresh attempt was made to initiate a deep water ferry link between Minehead and South Wales. Minehead's Coastal Town's Initiative (CTI) was launched by a former director of Butlin's Minehead, who was about to re-open discussions with the Welsh Development Agency about attracting more visitors to and from West Somerset from across the Bristol Channel. A Pier or jetty would need to be constructed.

On the 3rd September 2001 *M.V. Balmoral* sailed the Exmoor Coast down to Ilfracombe and Lundy Island.

On the 20th October 2001 *P.S. Waverley* back after her £4m refit sailed over to Cardiff for a shopping spree.

The Western Economic Development & Access (WEDA) strategy, costing £37,000 was drawn up to identify and develop such schemes to improve the social and economic life of the town. The Strategy involved a wide range of agencies including the Somerset County Council, Exmoor National Park Authority and the government's flagship economic quango the South West Regional Development Agency (SWRDA). Also, in

January 2003, it was announced that the design work had begun on Part 2 of the Eden Project in Cornwall. The next stage of the development was expected to cost £75 million (almost as much as the original project). A feasibility study to decide whether such an expansion was possible would cost around £2.85 million, up to half of which would be funded by none other than the South West Regional Development Agency.

Some significant grants made during 2002/3 included:-

Falmouth Maritime Museum	£8.8 m
Plymouth Single Regeneration Budget	£6.8 m
St Austell Town Centre	£2.8 m
Royal William Yard	£4.7 m
RNAS Portland	£6.0 m
Millbay Docks	£4.8 m
Bristol Arena	£3.8 m
Eden Project	£2.8 m

The agency budget for 2003/4 was £131.4 million and 2005/6 £138.8 million. What were the chances for Minehead's CTI?

In July 2004 the owner of what is left of the Old Victorian pier at Quay West was passing Selworthy Sands in his fishing boat the *Scooby Doo 2* and radioed the inshore lifeboat for help to take a man and an injured dog off the beach.

In October 2004 two coach crashes blocked the A39 for four hours after two separate accidents. There was a need for something to complement the *West Somerset Railway*.

On the 17th June 2005 the P.S *Waverley* set sail along the Exmoor coast to Porlock Bay in honour of the men who served aboard paddle steamers in WWII. Many local men went to war with the White Funnel paddle steamers. They were joined by the Penarth Mail Voice Choir singing popular songs of the war years.

A survey carried out in June by the campaigning action group DIRECT supported the idea of building a pier with ferry services to Wales.

In September the Devon County Council gave their backing for a cross-channel ferry from Ilfracombe to Swansea (25 miles).

Another Call for a Ferry Link

On the 26th May 2006 another call for a ferry link to be set up between Minehead and South Wales was made by a marine consultant. Chris Marrow from Wellington has produced a feasibility study which he believes proves a link would be financially viable. It was envisaged a ferry could run between Minehead and Barry saving tourists a 125 mile round trip (via the M4/M5/A39) to the resort.

In March 2007 Mr. Marrow met business leaders to discuss funding for a fast catamaran ferry service, it was *when*, not *if*.

86 – Ferry project leader Chris Marrow is pictured on the Mumbles Pier, with the lifeboat station behind him, which would be the ferry landing site for Swansea

April 2008 – economic and shipping experts had thrown their weight behind plans to launch a ferry service between West Somerset, North Devon and South Wales. Professor Alf Baird, Head of the Marine Research Group at Edinburgh Napier University, claims such a link was inevitable, while leading Welsh business academic Professor Brian Morgan from the Cardiff School of Management at the University of Wales had billed the business plan as 'robust'.

Councilor Michael Dawes, West Somerset Council's economic portfolio holder said "a cross Bristol Channel ferry had the potential to open up new tourism opportunities for West Somerset. The cost of the project - £6M.

During April a second world war mine was washed up near Hinkley Point nuclear power station at Bridgewater and was detonated in a controlled explosion by the Royal Navy.

87 The type of vessel Chris Marrow of Severn Seas Ferries Co. hoped to use for the 35 minute journey between Minehead and Penarth. Built in 1996 with a top speed of 34 knots and a capacity of up to 350 passengers – Chris hoped to purchase the catamaran and its sister ship.

In August 2010 *"Severn Link"* Chairman, Chris Marrow reported the link between Minehead and Cardiff could go ahead next year, but with logistical problems at Swansea due to berthing, the ferry link was delayed.

Fresh Look at Feasibility of Ferry to West Somerset Link

In May 2012, Councilor Lillis, West Somerset Council, had been part of the Town Council led working group that had re-examined the ferry proposal which would cost up to £35K. The Authority's Amenities and General Purposes Committee recommended the Council seek funding from LARC (Local Action for Rural Communities) of £15K. It was hoped the Vale of Glamorgan Council would price-match. The study would not cost the Authority one penny. The scheme would involve constructing a pier/jetty at both Barry and Minehead.

The 6th of June 2012 (the anniversary of D-Day) turned out to be "Disappointment Day". At a meeting of the full Minehead Town Council only 10 councilors were present and seven members of the public. Earlier two local NIMBY's and one near-sighted

Councilor spoke against the proposed funding bid from LARC. Three councilors voted for the proposal and six against. The Mayor did not vote.

West Somerset Councilor Richard Lillis said later he, and others involved in the original proposal, would now contact LARC to find another way a funding bid could be made. He did not believe the idea was "dead in the water" and hoped it was not the end.

Angry Passengers

On the 5th of September 2012 PS *Waverley* failed to make a scheduled stop at Minehead for a trip to Ilfracombe and Lundy. Fifty passengers were left "high and dry" because the sailing had been "cancelled for operational reasons."

Vision Manager

In January 2013 the Minehead Visioning Group (part of the Minehead Development Trust) had appointed the first Vision Manager (Town Centre Manager), Mr Stephen Hooper who had previously worked in South Wales. Perhaps one of his first "visions" will be to promote the Minehead to Barry ferry link.

In February Clevedon pier was awarded £500K for another refurbishment from the Coastal Communities Fund.

The £30B Severn Barrage hydro electricity scheme had been rejected, It was to include a dual carriageway and a light railway from Brean Down to Lavernock Point. In 2007 it was suggested the site be moved to Minehead to increase the power output. Why not use the money for a tunnel instead, to link the Glamorgan Heritage Coast with the Exmoor Heritage Coast? It would also take the pressure off the M5 and A39 road systems.

For comparison, the Channel Tunnel under the Engish Channel which opened in 1994 took 6 years to build, is 32 miles long and cost £4.6B. A new Severn tunnel should be a less onerous undertaking.

CONCLUSION

Gateway To Exmoor

There are two approaches to Minehead, both impressive. The first is by road, from the East, along the A39. As one turns the corner at Big Firs, between Carhampton and Dunster, towards the town, the back-drop of the North Hill and camp ground is enticing and welcoming. The second is by sea, seldom seen these days, from the Bristol Channel. As the bow of the steamer crosses the Bridgwater Bar and points toward St Michael's church tower (where once upon a time lamps were lit to help guide seafarers safely into harbour) the view is simply breathtaking. The North Hill once again standing prominently to starboard with Dunkery straight ahead, in the distance and Grabbist to the port side completing the panoramic landscape. It is easily understood why Minehead is known as the *'Gateway to Exmoor'* or sometimes the *'Sea Gate of Exmoor.'* It is the ideal centre for walking in the *National Park*, the *Coleridge Way* and the *South West Coastal Path*.

88 - Minehead – Gateway to Exmoor

We should all be thankful for the Paddle Steamer Preservation Society who ensures the legacy of Minehead pier is not forgotten by still operating the *Waverley* and *Balmoral* carrying on the great tradition of day trips and afternoon cruises from Minehead that first began in Victorian days. Also, to those who, since the end of the war, have tried to get the pier replaced.

Every resident and visitor to West Somerset should at least once in their lifetime, take an afternoon cruise along the Exmoor coast, visit Ilfracombe and Lundy Island or maybe cross the Bristol Channel to South Wales and take a closer look at the Welsh mountains or visit Holm Islands and see Clevedon Pier. A unique experience for all the family. Captain Andy Obrian, skipper of the *P.S. Waverley* says there is no better way to spend the day than relaxing on deck and watching the spectacular scenery slip by.

You may decide to become a member of the PSPS and join many thousands who each summer 'look for the adventure that they crave' and finds its reward.

A Few Facts

1744 –   Charles Wesley's brother John, after preaching to Minehead residents on the sea shore, crossed over to South Wales in a sloop taking only 4 hours.

1861 –   A boat the "Jane and Susan" sailed from Minehead to Bristol (Welsh Back) in 4 hours 48 minutes.

1912 –   A paddle steamer crossed the 20 miles from Cardiff to Minehead in 1 hour 45 minutes - 93 miles by road taking approximately 2½ hours today.

1923 –   The paddle steamer *Glen Gower* held the record for crossing from Ilfracombe to Swansea, 25 miles in 1 hour 16 minutes – a 4 hour drive by road today.

1957 –   P.S. *Glen Gower* took only 1½ hours to cross the 18 miles to Minehead.

1998 –   72 out of 87 coaches (83%) visited Minehead from the Welsh coast via the M5 and A39 roads.

2000 –   25% of visitors to Minehead Butlins (Somerwest World) come from South Wales across the Channel to Minehead by sea, a 1 hour trip by 'ferry'. Compared with 93 miles by road taking 2½ hours.

2003 –   Appledore shipyard closed through lack of orders.

2004 –   Three new Torpoint ferries are being built in Glasgow, Plym II, Lynher II and Tamar II (73 cars each).

2005 –   Rowers from Watchet cross the 18 miles from Barry in 3 hours 45 minutes.

2006 –   A windsurfer crossed (accidentally) from Swansea to Woody Bay in 3 hours.

Acknowledgements and Bibliography

Dunster Castle Muniments

Somerset Record Office

West Somerset Free Press 'Notes'

Hilary Binding and Doug Stevens, The Book of Minehead with Alcombe

Donald Brown, Somerset v. Hitler

Chris Collard, On Admiralty Service

Chris Collard, P & A Campbell's Pleasure Steamers 1887-1945

Chris Collard, White Funnels – Vol 2

Bernard Cox, Pleasure Steamers

Graham Farr, West Country Passenger Steamers

Caroline J Giddens, Minehead, a Little History

John Gilman, Exmoor's Maritime Heritage

Jack Greaves, R.N.L.I. Minehead, 1901-2001, The First 100 Years

Jack Hurley, Exmoor in Wartime

Lois Lamplugh, Minehead and Dunster

Colin Russell, Lecture notes on Minehead Harbour and Pier

Mike Telstone, Paddle Steamer Preservation Society

S.I.A.S. Survey No 14

Sean Wilson

List of Illustrations

The Paddle Steamer Preservation Society

The Paddle Steamer Preservation Society is Britain's longest established, largest and most successful steamship preservation group. It is a registered charity and, through their associated charitable and non-profit making companies, operate Britain's only two working passenger paddle steamers *Waverley* and *Kingswear Castle* – both of which have won major heritage awards. They also fully support the operation of the M.V. *Balmoral.*

The society offers a range of attractive facilities to members including discount cruising vouchers, free tickets for children, quarterly magazines for members and junior members and regular branch meetings held in centres throughout the country. The Bristol Channel Branch is particularly active and friendly, both on board during the summer and at frequent meetings in Cardiff and Bristol. For full information about the society write to PSPS, P. O. Box 365, Worcester WR3 7WH.

Details of excursions are available from Waverley Excursions, Glasgow 0141-243-2224 where bookings can be made. Tickets can also be purchased on board from the purser. You can also obtain tickets from Tourist Information Centres at Bridgwater, Minehead and Taunton or book on line at www.waverleyexcursions.co.uk.

About The Author

Charles was born in Summerland Avenue, Minehead in 1936. He went to the infant school in Mddle Street (Head Teacher Miss Cross) and then on to the Boy's School in Watery Lane (Head Teacher Mr Chant). On leaving school he joined the Post Office as a Telegram Boy and later as a Postman. He was a chorister at St Andrews and St Michael's Churches. As a Queen Scout in the 3rd Minehead troop he represented Somerset at Windsor Castle in 1954.

Following National Service he rejoined the Post Office and was promoted to Postal & Telegraph Officer and "posted" to Glastonbury. He was later transferred to Taunton H.P.O.

In 1960 he married Shirley, a local girl, at St Michael's Church. They have two children, Christopher and Helen, and four grandchildren, Matthew, Alex, Kieran and Naomi.

In 1968 an opportunity arose to move to the Telephony side of the P.O. and Charles moved to Exeter. After 25 years he took voluntary redundancy and worked for the Exeter City Council as one of the Voluntary Red Coat City Guides. Five years later he took a position as Relief Mace Sergeant at the Guildhall where he worked as part of the Lord Mayor's support team. In 2008 he finally hung up his mace and retired for good.

Six years ago he decided to retire to West Somerset and now lives in Minehead again.

CPSIA information can be obtained at www.ICGtesting.com
Printed in the USA
LVOW02s0844211114

3774LVUK00017B/4/P